THE SEVEN
SORROWS
OF *Mary*

THE SEVEN SORROWS OF Mary

Romanus Cessario, O.P.

MAGNIFICAT

Paris · New York · Madrid · Oxford

Publisher: Pierre-Marie Dumont
Editor: Romain Lizé
Copy editor: Susan Needham
Iconography: Isabelle Mascaras
Layout: Élise Borel
Production: Thierry Dubus, Sabine Marioni
Concept and Design: MAGNIFICAT (Romain Lizé, Marthe Rollier)
Proofreader: Janet Chevrier

Artworks:
The Presentation of the Virgin in the Temple (p. 9), *The Presentation of Jesus in the Temple* (p. 13), *The Flight into Egypt* (p. 23), *Jesus with the Doctors in the Temple* (p. 33), *The Carrying of the Cross to Calvary* (p. 43), *The Crucifixion* (p. 53), *The Deposition of Christ* (p. 63), frescoes (1304-1305), Giotto di Bondone (1266-1336), Scrovegni Chapel, Padua, Italy. © The Art Archive / Scrovegni Chapel Padua / A. Dagli Orti.
The Entombment of Christ (p. 73), *The Deposition of Christ* (p. 83), frescoes (c. 1325-1330), Pietro Lorenzetti (v. 1280-v. 1348), Basilica of St Francis, Assisi, Italy. © akg-images / Stefan Diller. © akg-images / De Agostini Pict. Lib.

ISBN: 978-1-936260-91-1
First edition: February 2014
Printed by Transcontinental, Canada
Photo engraving: Aquatre, Paris
© MAGNIFICAT. All rights reserved.

CONTENTS

For

Robert Augustine Twele, O.F.M. CONV. (1981)
Peter John Cameron, O.P. (1986)
John Albert Langlois, O.P. (1991)
George Philip Mary Schommer, O.P. (1994)
Andrew More O'Connor (1996)
Jeremy St. Martin (2002)
Aquinas Guilbeau, O.P. (2002)
Paul Henry Dumais (2004)
Mark Barr (2008)
Huy Nguyen (2009)
Ryan Wilson Connors (2012)
Reginald Lynch, O.P. (2013)
Cassian Derbes, O.P. (2014)
Cajetan Cuddy, O.P. (2014)

Who Act in the Person of Christ
Head, Shepherd, and Bridegroom

THE SEVEN SORROWS OF *Mary*

Illustrations from
Giotto di Bondone (1266-1336)
Scrovegni Chapel (Padua)
and
Pietro Lorenzetti (c. 1280-c. 1348)
Basilica of St. Francis (Assisi)

Foreword

In Mary, we contemplate at one and the same time the Creator's original project and his intent, that is, the salvation of mankind, a subject about which Saint Paul said: "He delivered us from the power of darkness and transferred us to the kingdom of his beloved Son" (Col 1:13). This is why Mary so attracts us and consoles us like no other human being. Her path is the model of the path for us to follow in order to attain mercy and make it our own.

Even if allusions to Mary in the New Testament are few and far between, they nevertheless provide access to the heart of the relationship between Jesus and Mary which, through "the analogy of faith," allows us to understand many things. Marian piety springs spontaneously from the heart. This piety is not "madness," but rather somewhat like the reaction of that woman in the crowd who calls out to Jesus: "Blessed is the womb that carried you and the breasts at which you nursed" (Lk 11:27). This woman admires Jesus and includes his mother in her admiration: what joy it must be to have such a son! Jesus' response seems abrupt: "Rather, blessed are those who hear the word of God and observe it" (Lk 11:28). Other words of Jesus regarding his mother seem just as harsh, as when, upon being told that his mother and brothers are outside, he replies: "Who is my mother? Who are my brothers? . . . Whoever does the will of my heavenly Father is my brother, and sister, and mother" (Mt 12:48-50). His words in the Temple at the age of twelve appear harsher still: "Why were you looking for me? Did you not know that I must be in my Father's house?" (Lk 2:49). And at Cana, he tells his mother: "Woman, how does your concern affect me? My hour has not yet come" (Jn 2:4).

Mary's reaction to these words of Jesus, which seem to rebuff her, shows how she "advanced in her pilgrimage of faith" (*Lumen Gentium*, 58). First, there is the fact, painfully expressed in Luke, that she does not understand: "But they [the parents of Jesus] did not understand what he said to them" (Lk 2:50). But there is also her docile, approving, submission, "Do whatever he tells you" (Jn 2:5), at the wedding at Cana. Jesus refers his listeners—as well as his mother—to the will of God. This is what the Christian life is all about. The will of God is Jesus' "food": "My food is to do the will of the one who sent me" (Jn 4:34). That is where he wishes to lead us: "Come and see!"

The path of the mother of Jesus is also: "May it be done to me according to your word" (Lk 1:38). Her path is the will of God, her total, undivided, gift of herself to God's will. That which at first appears as Jesus' lack of compassion toward his mother is in reality that path that they will travel together, the school of divine mercy. Mary must advance step by step along this path where Jesus leads her.

Popular piety understood all this, with the sensitivity and intuition of the heart, by meditating on the seven sorrows of the Virgin Mary, by suffering with her, by sharing her suffering.

Delving further still, we see that the heart of Mary is configured to the heart of her Son. Her Son's desire becomes her desire: the salvation of all men. It was for this that she abandoned all the spontaneous affection of her mother's heart and gave her Son complete freedom to accomplish his mission. Furthermore, she herself said yes to the Cross. This is why, at the foot of the Cross, Jesus made her the mother of all his disciples.

Such is the mystery of the "Mother of Mercy": at the foot of the Cross, she became "the refuge of sinners," of all those who, through their sins, killed (and are still killing) Jesus, he who died for their sins, he, "the Lamb of God who takes away the sins of the world."

Through this magnificent book, Father Romanus Cessario, O.P., makes us enter, like so many Christians before us, into the contemplation of the seven sorrows of the Virgin Mary. Through Mary, the Mother of Mercy, we are led to become merciful as our Father is merciful, and to welcome the mercy of Jesus into our hearts.

Christoph Cardinal Schönborn, O.P.
Archbishop of Vienna

INTRODUCTION

The Sorrows of the Blessed Virgin Mary occupy an established place within Christian liturgy, devotion, and art. A centuries-old custom identifies seven episodes in the life of the Mother of God as moments when Our Lady experienced blessed sorrow. The number seven of course designates all those times throughout her life when, before Christ's Resurrection, Mary shared the sorrows that, according to the plan of divine Providence, the Incarnation of the Son of God entailed. Six of these seven sorrowful events are recorded in the New Testament. One, the time when Mary meets Christ on the road to Calvary, finds biblical warrant in the Song of Songs:

Daughters of Jerusalem, go out
and look upon King Solomon

In the crown with which his mother has crowned him
on the day of his marriage,
on the day of the joy of his heart.

(Sg 3:10–11)

The Christological meaning of this text comforts us with the assurance that within Christian living, movements of sorrow and joy do not exclude each other. As long as we remain this side of heaven, the two emotions can and oftentimes do run alongside each other. Great solace, however, arises in the hearts of believers from the knowledge that, at the consummation of a virtuous life, Christ "will wipe every tear from their eyes" (Rev 21:4).

Mary's Seven Sorrows result from the intimate and unique participation that she enjoys in the saving work of her Son. While we know that the Man of Sorrows opens up for the human race a beatific destiny that the First Parents forfeited by their sin, we know also that he accomplishes this mission by taking away the sins of the world. Thus, we read in this striking phrase from Saint Paul: "For our sake he made him to be sin who did not know sin, so that we might become the righteousness of God in him" (2 Cor 5:21). Since no Christian may expect to enter God's glory without sorrowing here below, every follower of Christ will encounter moments in life when he or she must seek refuge with the *Mater Dolorosa*.

This volume completes a trilogy of meditations on the central mysteries of the Christian religion published by MAGNIFICAT. My earlier titles, *The Seven Last Words of Jesus* and *The Seven Joys of Mary*,

appeared in 2009 and 2011, respectively. The Catholic priest receives a special commission to preach those truths or mysteries that God has revealed for the salvation of the human race. With gratitude for the grace of our priestly perseverance, I have dedicated this little work on Mary's Seven Sorrows to the fourteen priests, some diocesan and some religious, who, during the past four decades, kindly have invited me to preach at their First Solemn Masses of Thanksgiving. These priests, according to the gifts and offices that each has received, continue to communicate Mary's joys and her sorrows to a world that stands deeply in need of a consolation that its inhabitants cannot expect to discover without aid.

THE FIRST SWORD: THE PROPHECY OF SIMEON

"And Simeon blessed them and said to Mary his mother, 'Behold, this child is destined for the fall and rise of many in Israel, and to be a sign that will be contradicted (and you yourself a sword will pierce) so that the thoughts of many hearts may be revealed.'"

(Lk 2:34–35)

The Blessed Virgin Mary participates in the redemptive mission of her Son, Our Lord Jesus Christ. This well-known axiom runs deep throughout Catholic teaching and life. In the last of the twentieth-century's major Church statements on Mary, we find papal confirmation of the place that Mary holds in the divine plan for our salvation: "Through faith the Mother shares in the death of her Son, in his redeeming death; but in contrast with the faith of the disciples who fled, hers was far more enlightened." Pope Saint John Paul II continues to explain this Marian mystery: "On Golgotha, Jesus through the Cross definitively confirmed that he was the 'sign of contradiction' foretold by Simeon. At the same time, there were also fulfilled on Golgotha the words which Simeon had addressed to Mary: 'and a sword will pierce through your own soul also.'"[1] Because of its biblical warrant, the sword that touches the Virgin Mother of God has become the pre-eminent symbol for the Seven Sorrows of Mary. To support this claim, we find depictions—icons and paintings—of Our Lady in which a sword pierces her heart. These images originate from within both Eastern and Western spheres of Christianity.

The Gospels record the circumstances that surround Christ's conception in the womb of the Blessed Virgin Mary. We know that the divine plan by which the Savior of the world enters into human history initially startled even Saint Joseph. That is, until "the angel of the Lord appeared to him in a dream and said, 'Joseph, son of David, do not be afraid to take Mary your wife into your home. For it is through the holy Spirit that this child has been conceived in her'" (Mt 1:20). The New Testament then pointedly describes the lowly estate of the Bethlehem manger. The joys of the Annunciation and of the Savior's birth already presage the self-emptying that the Son of God takes on himself and which he also establishes as a constitutive part of Christian living. Next comes the promise of a sword! The Presentation of the Lord, which the Church celebrates on 2 February, occasions Simeon's prophetic utter-

ance about the sufferings that God's plan for salvation in Christ entails. The sword spells death. Swords are for slaying. Swords destroy. What is the significance of Simeon's prophecy? The first sorrow that Our Lady endures announces the radical form of life that Catholic faith imposes on the baptized: "Or are you unaware that we who were baptized into Christ Jesus were baptized into his death?" (Rom 6:3).

Sometimes the most familiar truths escape our attention. One who enters a Catholic church immediately espies the image of the Crucified One. The Cross remains the symbol of the Christian religion throughout the world. Indeed, among the icons of world religions, only the Christian symbol finds its original explanation in the instrument of execution that the Roman world reserved for ignoble capital offenders. No other world religion holds up as emblematic of its belief a symbol that points immediately to death. The weapon of which Simeon spoke so as to alert Our Lady to her sorrows appears again in the New Testament. The symbol gives way to the reality, when, as Saint John recounts, the soldiers spared breaking Christ's legs (a practice meant to hasten the death of those crucified): "But when they came to Jesus and saw that he was already dead, they did not break his legs, but one soldier thrust his lance into his side, and immediately blood and water flowed out. An eyewitness has testified, and his testimony is true; he knows that he is speaking the truth, so that you also may [come to] believe" (Jn 19:33–35). Mary's first sorrow announces that no Christian escapes the embrace of the Cross and that no Christian heart survives without being pierced. For, as Oscar Wilde has plaintively observed of the human condition, "How else but through a broken heart, / May Lord Christ enter in."[2]

We cannot comprehend in faith the sorrows of Mary apart from remembering her joys. Nothing of the schizophrenic invades Catholic teaching and piety. Easter follows Good Friday. Because of the symmetry between joy and sorrow, the Christian tradition encourages preachers and believers alike to remember that the image of God in which every person on the planet is created seeks a twofold perfection in order to surpass the limitations of the cosmos. Because of human sin, the image of God requires restoration. Because of the new life, the spiritual life, that as far as we know only Baptism imparts, the image of God requires a super-added perfection we call grace. As gifts of divine grace, image restoration and image perfection, in their ongoing dynamic, remain inseparable throughout the life of the Christian believer. Sanitized, bourgeois, guilt-free Christianity produces only the illusion of well-being and of religious authenticity.

Mutant versions of the Gospel message produce bad religion. Those who skillfully assure listeners of their receiving spiritual rewards and of their enjoying divine approbation, though without also stressing conversion of life, still enjoy the power to fill large stadiums. At the same time, their promises ring hollow in the face of the oftentimes dramatic sorrows that befall the human race. Even were someone to escape life's greatest misfortunes, he or she must face death. And in the meantime, the apparently well off and carefree still experience that ache in the human heart that God has discreetly placed there to ensure that those whom he made for communion with him do not forget the God who made them. No wonder the Catholic tradition has incited its adherents to cultivate a devotion to

Our Lady of Sorrows. The world needs a Lady of Compassion who will console those who suffer from their own sins and those of others. In witness of this truth, Eastern Catholics celebrate Our Lady under the invocation of "She Who Softens Evil Hearts."[3] Significantly, the icon that represents the Mother of God under this provocative title shows Mary's heart pierced not by one but by seven swords.

In the explanation that accompanies the frontispiece for its Part Two, the *Catechism of the Catholic Church* teaches us: "The sacraments are as it were 'powers that go forth' from the Body of Christ to heal the wounds of sin and to give us the new life of Christ."[4] In recent catechetical literature and instruction, not much has been made of the sacraments as remedies for man's sinful condition. Theologians of an earlier period held a very different perspective on the sacraments of the Church. For example, the Dominican teacher of Saint Thomas Aquinas, Saint Albert the Great, "argued that [the seven sacraments] corresponded to the seven deadly sins and are designed as a remedy against them."[5] Today the Church herself continues to teach that the sacraments serve a remedial purpose within the practice of the Christian religion. At the same time, both Aquinas and the *Catechism* complement this instruction about image restoration by specifying the appropriate image perfections that each of the sacraments bestows on a devout recipient. While each sacrament confers a distinctive graced perfection, the overall effect of the various sacramental actions is what we call holiness. To put it differently, in the lapidary phrase of the first Encyclical Letter of Pope Francis, *Lumen fidei*, the sacraments, beginning with Baptism, effect a "transformation of our whole life in Christ."[6]

~

Because our meditation will follow those things that the Blessed Virgin Mary suffered during the course of her participation in the effecting or the bringing about of our salvation, we shall conclude each consideration of her Seven Sorrows with a specific sacramental instruction. The emphasis of these observations will be on how each sacrament heals the wounds of sin. What follows about the sacraments as remedies takes inspiration from the classical accounts of the Church's seven sacraments.[7] We will look at the rhythm of image restoration and image perfection, which no Christian can thwart without making out of his or her life the equivalent—to use a homely metaphor—of what happens during a Strauss waltz when one or the other of the dance-floor partners starts to move around the ballroom with, as the expression goes, two left feet.

Baptism supplies a remedy for the lack of a spiritual life that befalls all those born of woman. In this context, "spiritual life" means the Christian life. Pope Francis uses traditional language to describe the spiritual life when he assures us that "Christ's work penetrates the depths of our being and transforms us radically, making us adopted children of God and sharers in the divine nature."[8] No one can adopt himself, however. Saint Paul makes this clear when he reminds us that we have "received a spirit of adoption through which we cry, *Abba*, 'Father!'" (Rom 8: 15). To explain why only Baptism supplies a remedy for those deprived of a supernatural, spiritual life, evangelizers may have recourse to the following line of argumentation: No one can self-generate his or her own spiritual or Godly life. At best, individuals or societies manufacture religious simulacra which can only lead, ultimately, to either despair or mythology. Someone

who tells you that he or she successfully can block out all thought of God, and of some form of reckoning for their sins, is lying. Someone who claims to be spiritual but not religious is kidding himself. In short, an *apologia* for Baptism follows what reason can discover about God and about man's destiny.[9] Arguments of this kind may persuade an adult to admit the reasonableness of seeking Baptism, but only God's initiative can move a person to receive that sacrament which opens the door to the other sacraments. This means that we can only receive the "spirit of adoption" as a gift.

Baptism works powerfully. The potent transformation about which Pope Francis speaks results in a person being both configured and conformed to Christ. Configuration means that, once baptized, the Christian can never renounce or eradicate this sacramental bond or character. Conformity means that those who remain faithful to their baptismal graces enjoy intimacy with Christ.[10] So the first sorrow of Mary fittingly accompanies the first sacrament that the infant or the adult catechumen receives. As the Church proclaims, the newly baptized infant or adult rises from the baptismal bath radically transformed. At the same time, a lifetime of everyday challenges and temptations awaits even the baptized,

from whom this sacrament does not remove the here-and-now weaknesses that their First Parents discovered—all of a sudden—in the Garden (see Gen 3:7). The image of the piercing sword that Simeon used to forewarn Our Lady of her participation in Christ's Passion finds an analogous application in the condition of every Christian believer. No one escapes the "sword." In the face of this warning, however, Catholics find themselves in a privileged position. They know that, whatever sorrow they may encounter, there abides someone who, when it is needed, can soften evil hearts.

THE SECOND SWORD: THE FLIGHT INTO EGYPT

"When they had departed, behold, the angel of the Lord appeared to Joseph in a dream and said, 'Rise, take the child and his mother, flee to Egypt, and stay there until I tell you. Herod is going to search for the child to destroy him.'"

(Mt 2:13)

The Christian tradition clearly locates the Flight into Egypt within the divine plan of salvation. From their earliest reflections on the Gospel, the Church Fathers emphasized that this episode in the life of the newborn Redeemer requires the eyes of faith for its proper interpretation. In other words, we should not read about the Flight into Egypt and think to ourselves that somehow God nearly lost control of things. We should not wonder whether King Herod, who ordered the slaughter of the Holy Innocents, almost succeeded in snuffing out the life of the Incarnate Son of God. Nothing of the sort crosses the minds of those who read the Scriptures as testimonies of faith. Instead, the ancient commentators made it clear that Christ went down into Egypt to destroy idols and "to shine on those who dwell in darkness and the shadow of death" (Lk 1:79). Mary's faith tempered the sorrow that they "who are persecuted for the sake of righteousness" (Mt 5:10) must endure.

Sorrow arises from some kind of an encounter with evil. Many people find it difficult to grasp why God would allow evil to erupt in a world that remains firmly under the control of his Providence. For certain of our contemporaries, the beholding or attestation of evil, especially those evils perpetrated against the innocent, causes them to complain or mutter about God. Others even indict God. As C. S. Lewis expressed it, they put God in the dock.[1] Still other persons find in the eruption of evil a putative reason for denying the existence of an omnipotent, benevolent God. These outlooks can only distract the Christian believer from judging rightly about what some people term the *mysterium iniquitatis*, the mystery of evil. The Flight into Egypt, however, provides as good an occasion as any to help the Christian believer understand why God allows evil to erupt in the world. Herod's intentions were evil. He sought to kill the Christ Child, and he in fact slaughtered many baby boys, whom we venerate as saints. Herod committed evil deeds to secure his power. Saint Quodvultdeus, an early Church author, corrects the raging king: "Your throne is threatened by the source of grace—so small, yet so

great—who is lying in the manger. He is using you, all unaware of it, to work out his own purposes freeing souls from captivity to the devil. . . . But you, Herod, do not know this and are disturbed and furious. While you vent your fury against the child, you are already paying him homage, and do not know it."[2] The lesson: Evil never trumps God's power at work in the world.

The second sorrow of Mary associates her with those sufferings endured by persons whom we number among exiles, refugees, and migrants. At the same time, the many legends that have come down to us about the Flight into Egypt— for example, idols that crumble as the Holy Family passes by and fruit trees that droop down to provide easily for their sustenance — prompt us to discover in this second sword the hand of divine Providence. Since she enjoyed the enlightened faith to grasp how her sorrow fits into God's plan for our salvation, Mary courageously sustained her exile. No wonder the French artist Nicolas Poussin adorns his seventeenth-century oil painting of the Blessed Mother's second sorrow with a luminous guiding angel that hovers over Jesus, Mary, and Joseph as they journey through the pharaonic lands.[3]

In his book *The Seven Swords*, the twentieth-century Dominican author Father Gerald Vann observes that "St. Thomas says of the flight into Egypt: 'He [Christ] willed this flight that he might thereby bring back those who flee from the face of God.'"[4] People ordinarily flee from those whom they fear. Fear results from one's encounter with evil. How could any person fear the God who is Goodness itself? Still, we number among the gifts of the Holy Spirit a divine movement called Fear of the Lord. In its most virtuous expression, this gift characterizes the person who fears committing sin, that is, moral evil: who fears it for no reason other than his or her attachment to the divine Goodness. In other words, filial fear — the kind of fear that distinguishes those who are rightly called God's sons and daughters — moves a person to a virtuous fear, not of punishment, but of the very thought of offending the Good God.

Catholic theology also acknowledges other kinds of fear of God.[5] For the person who regards God only as One who can inflict punishment, the bestowal of filial fear awaits the conversion of their hearts. King Herod, for instance, exemplifies a man of what we call worldly fear. Worldly fear describes the state of a person who is trapped in sin, that is, one who prefers to embrace the punishments that sin incurs instead of fleeing them.[6] Herod dies a murderer. Servile fear, on the other hand, characterizes the man who accepts as true what the *Catechism* teaches about the Ten Commandments and therefore struggles to avoid incurring the punishments that violating them imposes. The man of servile fear still experiences the tugs and pulls of passion

and may even wish that there were available to him a guiltless form of sinning. Because, however, he recognizes the risks both of temporal punishments—for example, being caught by someone, doing prison time, loss of self-respect, etc.—and of eternal punishments, i.e., hell, the man of servile fear strives to avoid sinning. This servile posture, though, remains intrinsically fragile. To the extent that such striving is not referred to the love of God, servile fear—especially in today's culture where many have forgotten about God—gives way easily to servility or slavishness. In a word, the man of servility neither loves nor hates; he only fears like a slave and slowly grows indignant because of the constraint that he imagines that God's law imposes on him.

We can discern two kinds of evils. There are those evils that we suffer; there are also those that we commit. We call the latter actual sins. Sometimes the evil that we suffer results from the sins that we commit. The Flight into Egypt, as Saint Thomas Aquinas reminds us, warns us about making the land of darkness and of idols a permanent residence. When we experience the sorrow that arises from our sins, we should not blame God or call him to task. Instead, Mary's second sorrow encourages us to remember that she, with the Christ Child and with Saint Joseph, went down into Egypt so that those who are tempted to flee from the face of God might make a turnabout and return to Him.

Confirmation supplies a remedy against the weakness to which youths are subject for a period of time.[7] In the recent past, young men and women were told that they should think of themselves as soldiers serving in Christ's army. Today, most observers would grant that the "period of time" during which young people require special strengthening against the perils of contemporary culture lasts longer in the twenty-first century than it did in earlier eras of the Church's history. The practice of the Western Church of administering Confirmation after a child has reached the age of discretion acknowledges that young Christians require special catechetical instruction and the time to mature in the Christian life before they undertake Christian witness outside the supports that one ordinarily expects to find in their families. Young Christian soldiers must step out into the public arena, and they must also contend with the ambiguities that they encounter there. Because of their natural-law inclinations for raising children, parents spontaneously recognize that their children at a certain point in their maturation require further instruction in ethical and religious practices. Even though Confirmation classes still draw candidates, those responsible for instruction find it challenging to communicate the seriousness of Christian commitment, especially the observance of its sacramental rhythms. This circumstance proves especially regrettable when we learn that in 2010, more people age thirty-five to sixty-four died in the United States from suicide than from automobile accidents.[8] While this startling statistic can serve to support the general approach to the sacraments as remedies for the harmful effects of sin, it especially points up the need for teaching young people how to sustain their sorrows in a Godly manner. They also require instruction on how to avoid the expedient resolutions that can more easily exacerbate than resolve their personal difficulties. Soldiering for Christ requires a period of intense formation during which the young person learns the radical character of Christian life and faith.

The Flight into Egypt introduces a traditional theme in the

spiritual life of Christians that over the past fifty years has undergone a certain eclipse. Christian living requires a kind of *fuga mundi* or flight from the world. We find among the first saints of the Church men such as the fourth-century figure Anthony of the Desert. He maintained for three-quarters of a century a more or less solitary life, that is, the

life of a hermit, in the environs of the Nile River. Although his reputation drew followers, these disciples also were obliged to flee the civilized world of their age. Egyptian monasticism still instructs the Church. God, of course, does not ordain that the majority of Christian believers emulate Saint Anthony's complete withdrawal from the world. At the same time, this Egyptian saint's example sets a certain standard of life for Christians, even for young Christians. Confirmation preparation affords them the opportunity to learn how to adapt a rigorous *fuga mundi* to their circumstances in life. Confirmation promises a special outpouring of the gifts of the Holy Spirit. It is difficult, however, to imagine how these movements of the Holy Spirit that act upon the docile soul can arrive, let alone survive, in a person who remains fully enmeshed in the rhythms and hustle-bustle of contemporary secular life.

Saint Paul urges all Christians to depart from worldly standards: "Do not conform yourselves to this age but be transformed by the renewal of your mind, that you may discern what is the will of God, what is good and pleasing and perfect" (Rom 12:2). Saint Anthony of the Desert stands out as a principal patron for Christian asceticism. The young Catholic, in preparing to receive the Sacrament of Confirmation, should come to realize that his or her commitment to the practice of the Christian religion cannot coexist with attachment to every fashion and style

that the secular culture holds up for emulation. While generalizations are difficult to make, some examples of departure from worldly ways of living include paying special attention to the needs of the poor, resisting secular ethical outlooks that conflict sharply with revealed moral truth, and observing faithfully the actions that the virtue of religion obliges all human creatures to render to God, especially fidelity to personal prayer and cultivation of a devout spirit. No one gains stability in Christian maturity without practicing some form of asceticism, without in some way leaving the world, even if, as happens in the case of most Christian believers, one is obliged to dwell within its visible confines. In other words, everyone is called to share the second sorrow of Mary. When they do, they will appreciate the prophetic meaning that Saint Matthew attaches to the Flight into Egypt: "Joseph rose and took the child and his mother by night and departed for Egypt. He stayed there until the death of Herod, that what the Lord had said through the prophet might be fulfilled, 'Out of Egypt I called my son'" (Mt 2:14–15).

The Third Sword: The Loss of the Child Jesus in the Temple

"After they had completed [the feast's] days, as they were returning, the boy Jesus remained behind in Jerusalem, but his parents did not know it. Thinking that he was in the caravan, they journeyed for a day and looked for him among their relatives and acquaintances, but not finding him, they returned to Jerusalem to look for him."

(Lk 2:43–45)

nitially, Mary's third sorrow baffles the New Testament reader who seeks to discover what saving truth this apparently quixotic deed of the youthful Christ is meant to reveal. The sorrows that attended the infancy of Christ arose either from what Simeon said about the Child or what Herod sought to inflict on the Child. Mary's third sorrow, however, comes as a result of the blessed Child's own initiative: he stayed behind in Jerusalem in the company of the official teachers of the Old Testament. What may one think about this seeming disregard for the parental diligence that Mary and Joseph exercised faithfully while caring for the Incarnate Son of God? First of all, one may not

think ill of Our Lord. The Christian believer therefore resists all temptations to interpret Mary's third sorrow as caused by the negligence or, still less, by the rebelliousness of her twelve-year-old Child. The One who saves the human race from its sin himself cannot participate in the sins that men commit. Christian faith requires that we seek another explanation of this sorrow caused by the loss of the Child Jesus.

In order to discover the saving truth that the third sorrow teaches us, we need to remember what the faith communicates to us about Christ. What accounts for the sinlessness and impeccability of the Incarnate Son of God? In a word, it is the unique status that the humanity of Christ enjoys among all creatures. From the moment of his conception, Christ receives a plenitude of grace that belongs uniquely to the One whose humanity finds its subsistence in a Divine Person. In order to appreciate this mystery, human understanding must give way to divine faith. This surrender occurs each Sunday when, at Mass, we profess the Creed: this youthful Child who stays back in the Temple remains "God from God, Light from Light, true God from true God."[1] It would make no sense to imagine that the Incarnate Son of God decided, at a certain juncture in his life, to inflict sorrow on his Mother. No, like all of Mary's sorrows, the third sorrow unites her to the salvific mission of her Son. Her third sorrow draws her close to the twelve-year-old Christ

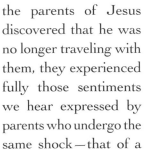

Child not as a delinquent but as the Savior of the world, who must be in his Father's house (see Lk 2:49).

The third sorrow illustrates Mary's enlightened faith. When the parents of Jesus discovered that he was no longer traveling with them, they experienced fully those sentiments we hear expressed by parents who undergo the same shock—that of a missing child. Mary's sorrows cannot be reduced to rhetorical devices that authors use to provide palliative care for a broken world. Mary underwent a true sorrow associated with the "anxiety" (Lk 2:48) that arises from discovering that a child is missing. It would be wrongheaded, at the same time, to interpret this mystery in Jesus' life as one that finds its saving meaning embodied in a heightened dramatic narrative: Panicked Mother Looks for Lost Child. God's drama produces a different kind of tension than what arises when playwrights set before us their *dramatis personae* caught in stark contrasts between good and evil. The ancient Greeks, for example, produced such tragedies. God brings forth only those works that flow from his wise and loving Providence. For those who succumb willingly to the rhythms of God's plan for their lives—in short, for those who remain faithful to the seven sacraments of salvation—only one destiny awaits them. We call it heaven. For the person who abides in God's Providence, who looks for the signs—even the little signs—that a loving Providence provides, the alternatives in life do not reduce themselves to either a depressive pessimism or an irony-tinted escapism. Those persons who live by Christian faith "know that all things work for good for those who love God, who are called according to his purpose" (Rom 8:28). Mary's third sorrow sets before us a living example of this foundational principle of Christian living.

Providence sometimes works quickly. The third sorrow that Mary endures as she hastens back to Jerusalem to look for what she may have considered to be a lost Child turns into one of Mary's joys. The joyful mysteries of the Rosary, for example, include the Finding in the Temple. Christian teaching assures us that joy and sorrow can coexist in the person who has committed himself or herself to God's providential care. In short, joy and sorrow blend in all those who pray devoutly the Our Father. What evidence do we have for this assertion? Consider how Saint Luke presents the loss of the Child Jesus. When he recounts this episode in the life of Christ, the Gospel text is noticeable for its sobriety and discretion. The only comment

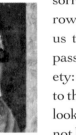

that Our Lady makes about her psychological dispositions underscores the seriousness with which she and Saint Joseph sought the lost Child: "Son, why have you done this to us? Your father and I have been looking for you with great anxiety" (Lk 2:48). Saint Luke, however, chooses not to supply a commentary on Our Lady's emotional state, even though the tradition gives Saint Luke a special affinity with the Mother of the Savior. He is said to have painted her image! Why this discretion? The Gospel points us immediately to the providential aspect of Mary's third sorrow. Our Lady's sorrow-turned-joy points us to a truth that surpasses a mother's anxiety: "And [Jesus] said to them, 'Why were you looking for me? Did you not know that I must be in my Father's house?'" (Lk 2:49).

Mary's third sorrow especially commits us to ponder the divine delicatesse. We need tutoring in the ways in which divine Providence works. The Letter to the Ephesians urges Christians to "be renewed in the spirit of your minds" (Eph 4:23). This requires that we accustom ourselves to look at things from God's perspective. Critics of Christianity often levy the charge that to follow this Gospel injunction reduces the free person to a state of dependence on others. Or, they allege that surrender to God leaves Christians ill-suited for developing self-initiative. In other words, secular critics smirkingly insinuate that surrendering oneself to the divine suavity reduces the free agent to a state of submissiveness. These critics, however, have failed to grasp how God rules the world he has made. They regard God as an impersonal power instead of as a loving Father. These same critics, whether they know it or not, find themselves confined to the narrow world of those ancient dramatists who could conceive of human life only in terms of tragedies—oftentimes instigated if not perpetrated by anthropomorphized gods who used

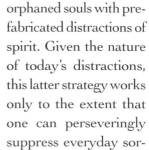

their superpowers to wreak vengeance on a hapless humanity—or comedies in which, since life's sorrows serve no apparently meaningful purpose, comic actors must entertain orphaned souls with prefabricated distractions of spirit. Given the nature of today's distractions, this latter strategy works only to the extent that one can perseveringly suppress everyday sorrows. As Miss Ella Fitzgerald in "Get Happy" sang, "Forget your troubles, c'mon get happy / Ya better chase all your cares away."[2]

The saints provide the best examples of those who recognize what it means to experience at the same time bitter sufferings and spiritual joys. Saint Thérèse of the Child Jesus reports that when she heard a priest explain how Christ in the

Garden experienced at the same time both the utmost agony and the highest spiritual joy, she innocently (and in a way that is self-revealing about her interior life) remarked that she understood how this could happen to Our Lord. She herself, so reports the Little Flower of Lisieux, underwent similar simultaneous desolations and consolations.[3] The lesson that Thérèse teaches us does not concern only pious souls who cultivate spiritual dispositions and who then retire from the world of human attachments. Lisieux teaches the world. When we hear people complain about suffering, we should remind them of something: the only thing worse than what they suffer would be to endure suffering apart from a deep attachment to God's love.[4] That

is, to suffer without faith, hope, and charity. No wonder Pope Francis calls the theological virtues the "driving force of the Christian life."[5]

The Blessed Eucharist requires us to mistrust appearances. Our senses perceive all the signs that appear proper to bread and wine, whereas our eyes of faith behold the substance of the Lord. The Church teaches us to respond to the Eucharistic conversion—what in technical language we call transubstantiation—by proclaiming a mystery of faith. This mystery dominates our whole lives. By joining in the Eucharistic sacrifice and by receiving Holy Communion, we discover how to adjust our mental habits to distinguish what appears from what really exists under the appearances of bread and wine. The Catholic believer needs to adapt this basic intuition of the Christian religion to his or her everyday life. We are not called to sustain a pollyannaish optimism, that is, to behave as if every sorrow were only an illusion. Christians adhere to realism. At the same time, we are required to judge our lives according to the same mystery of faith that we avow before receiving Holy Communion. When the priest puts the consecrated wafer on the tongue or in the hand of the recipient and says, "The Body of Christ," the communicant replies, "Amen." Mary's sorrows sustain believers throughout their lives, as they repeatedly say, "Amen," in response to the designs of a provident and loving God.

The Holy Eucharist is also remedial. Those who think of the Eucharist only as a joyful celebration might wonder how Holy Communion supplies a remedy against sin. Following a long tradition, the saints teach that receiving Holy Communion strengthens the communicant against his proneness to sin; Saint Thomas Aquinas quotes Saint Ambrose, "'this our daily bread is taken as a remedy against daily infirmity.'"[6] The sacred host is not a spiritual antibiotic. Devout reception of the Eucharist forgives venial sins. Why? Because the *res* or interior grace of the sacrament emerges as charity—"in act." In short, Holy Communion enkindles charity. What does this mean within the context of our meditation on the sorrows of

Mary? The more we love God, the better do we find ourselves capable of succumbing to his wise and loving Providence—in other words, the more do we find that our joys ease our sorrows.

No person who has witnessed even one Catholic Mass can fail to understand that the Eucharist remains intimately connected with the death of Christ. The words whereby the priest transforms the ordinary elements of bread and wine into the Body, Blood, soul, and divinity of Jesus Christ always begin with some reference to the night before he died. More needs to be said: the Last Supper and Calvary belong together. The eighteenth-century French bishop and spiritual author Jacques-Bénigne Bossuet uses the metaphor of the sword to represent the mystery of immolation or of the slaying—both physical and mystical—that stands at the heart of our redemption. He allegorizes the double consecration of the bread and of the wine by referring to a mystical sword that the priest wields when sacramentally he enacts the Eucharistic sacrifice.[7] The Christ whose death is re-enacted in the Eucharist also feeds us with his Body and Blood. Holy Communion makes us better lovers, not better mourners. Mary's third sorrow prepares us to ponder the sorrows that her Son endures in order to save the world, and to say Amen!

THE FOURTH SWORD: MARY MEETS JESUS ON THE WAY TO CALVARY

"Daughters of Jerusalem, go out and look upon King Solomon in the crown with which his mother has crowned him on the day of his marriage, on the day of the joy of his heart."

(Sg 3:10–11)

hough it is true that everything that the Lord Jesus Christ did and suffered during his sojourn on earth merits our salvation, nonetheless the New Testament makes it plain that the effective moment of Christ's redemptive merit and satisfaction occurs within the context of his Passion and death. It is quite difficult to read the four Gospels and to conclude that each narrative does not build up to the events that surround Good Friday. Mary's participation in the sorrows of her Son achieves a certain apex as Christ physically approaches the place of his death. Pope Saint John Paul II locates Mary's exquisite sorrow within the context of her uninterrupted journey of faith that does not spare her accompanying to Calvary him whom most around her regard as a condemned criminal: "From the moment of the Annunciation and conception, from the moment of his birth in the stable at Bethlehem, Mary followed Jesus step by step in her maternal pilgrimage of faith." The Pope continues: "She followed him during the years of his hidden life at Nazareth; she followed him also during the time after he left home, when he began 'to do and to teach' (cf. Acts 1:1) in the midst of Israel. Above all she followed him in the tragic experience of Golgotha."[1] With her enlightened faith, Mary follows Jesus everywhere. Now, as he mounts the way of the Cross, the *via crucis*, Mary steps forth from the mostly unenlightened onlookers that make up the crowd.

Although the Gospels do not explicitly mention Mary's encountering Christ on the way to Calvary, it is difficult to imagine that the women who stood at the foot of the Cross made no contact with Christ before he reached the summit, the Place of the Skull, Golgotha (see Jn 19:25). In any event, the traditional Stations of the Cross commemorate this encounter between Mother and Child as the Fourth Station. In 2012, Pope Benedict XVI commissioned a new set of meditations for the Good Friday devotions held each year at the Coliseum in Rome.[2] The authors drew on themes that, for centuries, holy men and women have developed as they pondered this poignant scene of Christ's catching a glimpse of his Mother along the road to Calvary. Here is what these twenty-first-century authors wrote: "On the way to Calvary, Jesus sees his mother. Their eyes meet. They understand one another. Mary knows who her son is. She knows whence he has come. She knows what his mission is. Mary knows that she is his mother; but she also knows that she is his daughter. She sees him suffer for all men and women, those of the past, present and future. And she too suffers."[3] Though the image of Mother and Child evokes one of the most intimate relationships that unite one person with another, Mary, through her enlightened faith, comes to appreciate more and more the universal significance of her Son's ascent to Calvary.

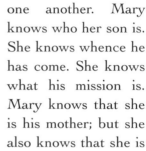

Christ mounts Calvary as a Bridegroom. When we interpret Mary's encounter with Christ along the *via crucis* according to the Song of Songs (which supplies the above-captioned scriptural foundation for Mary's fourth sorrow), we come to appreciate that for those who believe in divine Providence, their faith trumps the sorrow that arises when evil befalls them. The road to Calvary displays the dolorous circumstances that attend the Passion and death of the Redeemer. Still, God's saving plan remains at work. This truth of faith explains why Mary's fourth sorrow evokes a nuptial theme. Does comparing Christ's Calvary-ascent to a marriage procession risk one's mythologizing the sufferings of Jesus and the sorrows of Mary? We know

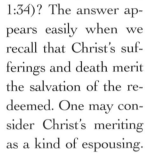

that Solomon represents Christ. But why should his wedding march foretell Mary's encounter with her suffering Son, who wears a crown of thorns, not one of royalty (see 1 Kg 1:34)? The answer appears easily when we recall that Christ's sufferings and death merit the salvation of the redeemed. One may consider Christ's meriting as a kind of espousing. To put it differently, the Church as Bride comes forth from the pierced side of Christ, the Bridegroom. So the *Catechism of the Catholic Church* teaches clearly: "The unity of Christ and the Church, head and members of one Body, also implies the distinction of the two within a personal relationship. This aspect is often expressed by the image of bridegroom and bride."[4]

Spiritual authors like to emphasize that while Mary sorrows genuinely, she never gives in to darkened sadness. Saint Thomas Aquinas helps us to understand this distinction. "Grief," he says, "regards the evil that is present."[5] One, however, may distinguish sadness (*tristitia*) from the emotion of pain or grief (*dolor*).[6] Popular usage does not always observe this nuance. For instance, the *Stabat Mater* in one English translation says of Mary: "O how sad and afflicted / was that blessed / Mother of her only-begotten Son."[7] At the same time, it is important to insist that the *Mater Dolorosa* experiences grief though never sadness. Indeed, how foreign to Christian sensibilities would the invocation "Mother Most Sad" sound to the ears of those who cherish Mary. This distinction also bears on our living the life of faith. Sadness befalls those who turn away from the Lord and his call. Thus, we read about the Rich Young Man in Saint Matthew's Gospel: "Jesus said to him, 'If you wish to be perfect, go, sell what you have and give to [the] poor, and you will have treasure in heaven. Then come, follow me.' When the young man heard this statement, he went away sad, for he had many possessions" (Mt 19:21–22). To put the teaching that Our Lady suffered grief but not sadness into simple terms, one could say that Our Lady's sorrow never blocked her overall vision of the heavenly treasures that her Son unlocked on Calvary.

Certain theologians have objected to artistic representations of Our Lady that depict her in a swoon or fainting spell.[8] While such images aim to capture something of the depth of Mary's sorrow, they at the same time communicate a message that Mary's sorrow—especially as Christ approached the place of his death—so completely overcame her that she could not contemplate any other reality. Mary, however, was not so overwhelmed by her sorrow that she forgot about God's plan to procure "treasure in heaven" (Mt 19:21) for an impoverished world. The classical images of Our Lady on Calvary actually depict her as standing upright and erect, with a sober though sorrowing mien. Again, these icons do not portray her so absorbed in grief that her emotions obscure the saving mystery in which she participates. Gerald Vann captures this basic truth of Marian devotion with clarity: "In [Mary] there are the two contradictory agonies: the longing to save him from his unbearable agony, the effort to help him finish his work; and it is the second that she must do, giving him to the world on the cross as she has given him to the world in the stable." Father Vann draws from Mary's fourth sorrow this important lesson for Christian loving and demeanor: "Human love helps when it is within the framework of vocation, when it expresses the will of God."[9] Because of the grace given to her, Mary's sorrow never gives way to sadness. Her personal agony does not paralyze her soul. We do not possess the same grace as does the Virgin Mother of God, the Immaculate One. However, Mary remains our most venerable Mother in the spiritual order. She therefore stands close by those whose sufferings incline them to sadness.

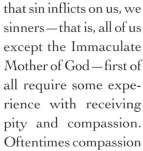

Christian devotion recognizes the image of Our Lady of Pity. There is something in human nature that identifies compassion with motherhood. A similar spiritual instinct drives those who find themselves caught up in dolorous circumstances to fly toward the person of Our Lady. Why? In the "Our Father," Christ instructs us to plead with God: "forgive us our debts, as we forgive our debtors" (Mt 6:12). While we usually can identify those who trespass against us, it is sometimes more difficult for Christians to acknowledge their own trespasses. Sin occasions both grief and sadness. In order to escape the ravages that sin inflicts on us, we sinners—that is, all of us except the Immaculate Mother of God—first of all require some experience with receiving pity and compassion. Oftentimes compassion does not emerge readily from others. Sometimes we find it difficult even to show true compassion to ourselves. These isolating moments direct the Christian believer to the Woman who exhibits the divine compassion or pity that accords perfectly with God's will. Thus, "Queen of the May," a traditional hymn sung at the May crownings of Our Lady's statue, makes us cry out:

"How dark without Mary / Life's journey would be."[10]

~

The Sacrament of Penance and Reconciliation affords an encounter where, through confession, contrition, and satisfaction, a penitent receives forgiveness for sins committed after Baptism. As instituted by Christ, this sacrament communicates efficaciously the divine pity. Two graces come to the penitent who confesses his or her sins. The fault of sin is removed, and so the serious sinner is restored to Eucharistic Communion — there being no other ordinary way to receive forgiveness for mortal sins.[11] The eternal punishment for sin is cancelled, though the debt of temporal punishment that sin incurs remains. "Absolution

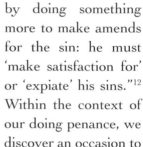

takes away sin," so teaches the Church, "but it does not remedy all the disorders sin has caused. Raised up from sin, the sinner must still recover his full spiritual health by doing something more to make amends for the sin: he must 'make satisfaction for' or 'expiate' his sins."[12] Within the context of our doing penance, we discover an occasion to have recourse to Our Lady of Pity. She gives us a balanced approach to our sinfulness, an approach that may be described negatively as neither falling into despair nor daring to presume on God's goodness and mercy.

Sometimes people wonder why they need to confess their sins to a priest. The answer to this question involves our recognizing that self-absolution creates an illusion. Catholic priests should find ways to explain to their congregations why the assurance of divine forgiveness that priests alone can pronounce authoritatively responds to the deepest inclinations of the moral conscience. Confession does not serve only the pious. Those who claim that they can live without forgiveness should under-

take a close reading of the Greek tragedies. The plays of Euripides, for example, portray what happens when men find themselves engaged in a vain effort to resolve deadly tensions, both internal and external, by appeal to human and cosmic powers alone.

Christian faith does not abandon its adherents to cosmic powers. The Christian believer clings rather to the Cross of Christ. Mary's encounter with her Son moves the French poet and dramatist Paul Claudel to recall a verse from the Song of Songs: "For my head is wet with dew, / my hair, with the moisture of the night" (Sg 5:2).[13] The Bride of the Song of Songs speaks these words, but the description refers to the state of the Bridegroom. Claudel interprets the "moisture of the night" as pointing to that night which Saint John mentions after the departure of Judas from the Cenacle: "So [Judas] took the morsel and left at once. And it was night" (Jn 13:30). The poet then ushers us into the shedding of Christ's blood that has brought to the whole world the grace of repentance.[14]

THE FIFTH SWORD: JESUS DIES ON THE CROSS

"When Jesus saw his mother and the disciple there whom he loved, he said to his mother, 'Woman, behold, your son.'"

(Jn 19:26)

The first stanza of the *Stabat Mater* commemorates the special meaning that Our Lady *juxta crucem*—by the Cross—holds for the Christian believer: "The mother stood sorrowing / by the cross, weeping / while her Son hung there."[1] The Second Vatican Council has authoritatively explained Catholic teaching on what Mary's standing near the Cross obtains for the human race.[2] Pope Saint John Paul II associates Mary's fifth sorrow with the prophecy that Elizabeth made at the Visitation concerning Mary's divine maternity: "'Blessed is she who believed.' This blessing reaches its full meaning when Mary stands beneath the Cross of her Son (cf. Jn. 19:25)." The Pope

continues: "The Council says that this happened 'not without a divine plan': by 'suffering deeply with her only-begotten Son and joining herself with her maternal spirit to his sacrifice, lovingly consenting to the immolation of the victim to whom she had given birth,' in this way Mary 'faithfully preserved her union with her Son even to the Cross.'"[3] The Church's liturgy praises this suavity of God: "In your wisdom and goodness the Blessed Virgin Mary, the mother and companion of the Redeemer, was to have a maternal role in the Church: of intercession and pardon, of prayer and grace, of reconciliation and peace."[4]

Mary did not stand alone on Calvary. As the Gospel recounts, with her there also stood the disciple whom Jesus loved. He is the Apostle John. When Jesus says, "Woman, behold, your son," the dying Savior, in fact, confides every Christian believer to the spiritual mediation of his Mother. This confiding of Mary to John emboldens Christian believers. They invoke Mary as Advocate, Auxiliatrix, Adjutrix, and Mediatrix.[5] These titles help us better to understand the wondrous exchange that Jesus enacts from the Cross. Christ gives his Mother to the disciple whom he loves, and we receive a treasure trove of spiritual mediations. "In effect, Mary's mediation," so the Church affirms, "is intimately linked with her motherhood. It possesses a specifically maternal character, which distinguishes it from the mediation of those other creatures

who in various and always subordinate ways share in the one mediation of Christ."[6] In other words, within the Church, Mary stands out as the first instrument of the One Mediator, and so, in some manner, participates in the other instruments whereby God bestows his grace on us.

Mary's place and work in the accomplishment of our salvation do not detract from the unique sacrifice of her Son. Like each created mediation that God has established within the Church of Christ, Mary "proclaims the greatness of the LORD" (Lk 1:46). Nothing created comes between God and his human creatures. Instead, the instruments that God uses to make us holy bring about not a separation or coming-in-between but, what one may call, a mediated immediacy. Christian authors metaphorically refer to Mary as the "neck" that unites Head and Body.[7] Christ's grace flows through Mary, who supernaturally connects the mystical Head with the members of his Body, the Church. This metaphor points up the organic unity of head, neck, and body. Many dramatic and not so dramatic conversion stories

confirm Mary's unique mediation in the Church. Conversion from sin of course depends on the Cross of the Savior and his merits; at the same time, sinners on the verge of conversion sense instinctively that the embrace of a mother awaits them. In 1939, the above-mentioned Paul Claudel, fifty years after his dramatic Christmas conversion at Notre Dame in Paris, captured this most Catholic of instincts when he exclaimed that "the day of Christ's consummation becomes the day of Mary's fulfillment."[8]

~

Many saints have helped the Christian people learn from Mary's sorrow at the death of her Son and her proximity to his moment of "consummation." Among them, the French diocesan priest Louis de Montfort (1673–1716) stands out as an exemplary teacher of this mystery. Papal affirmation supports this claim: "I would like to recall," writes Pope Saint John Paul II, "among the many witnesses and teachers of [Marian] spirituality, the figure of Saint Louis Marie Grignion de Montfort, who proposes consecration to Christ through the hands of Mary, as an effective means for Christians to live faithfully their baptismal commitments."[9] The saintly Pope's endorsement did much to restore to Marian devotion the writings of de Montfort, which had suffered a certain eclipse during the mid-twentieth century. Father de Montfort encouraged his hearers to regard

Our Lady as a channel of grace, and he proclaimed that no heavenly gift comes down to earth except through Our Lady.[10] The phrase that captures the teaching of Louis de Montfort remains familiar to many Catholics: *Ad Jesum per Mariam*. To Jesus through Mary.

De Montfort's Marian devotion aims to sustain the Christian in his or her "baptismal commit-

ments." These promises include our rejecting everything that runs contrary to Our Lady's soul and grace: "Do you renounce sin, so as to live in the freedom of the children of God? Do you renounce the lure of evil, so that sin may have no mastery over you? Do you reject Satan, the author and prince of sin?"[11] In the case of infant Baptism, the parents and godparents speak on behalf of the child about to be baptized. Those baptized as adults make these promises with full understanding of what they entail. Both infants (when, later, they reach the age of discretion) and adults when they leave the baptismal font discover that their maintaining these commitments requires fidelity. Temptation does not disappear from the world. Only a naive person ignores the challenges that everyday living brings forth. Our Lady's sorrows confirm the confidence that Christian believers place in her, especially at times of serious affliction and temptation. The familiar Marian prayer the *Memorare* includes this plea: "inspired with this confidence, / I fly to you, O Virgin of virgins, my Mother. / To you I come, before you I stand, sinful and sorrowful."[12] Since the first millennium, saints have encouraged sinners to seek refuge in the arms of the Blessed Virgin Mary. The Jesuit preacher Blessed Antonio Baldinucci (1665–1717) even spread devotion to Our Lady, Refuge of Sinners. To this day, the Catholic people receive

great consolation from knowing that Our Lady stands ready to receive them, whatever their state of fidelity to the promises made at Baptism.

Father Gerald Vann captures the consolation that Our Lady provides for those who share her participation in Christ's death. "We have to go down into his death," writes the author, "recognise the evil within us, the pride and the egoism, and recognise how they colour and taint all the things we do." In other words, we need to acknowledge our need for image restoration, for repentance after our failures to keep our baptismal promises. "Then," Father Vann continues, "in the nakedness of that self-knowledge we can give ourselves wholly into the hands of the Spirit and the Spirit can recreate us, for in the death of pride and egoism the soul is reborn as a child."[13] Saint Paul summarizes this interplay between image restoration and image perfection when he reminds the Romans: "The Spirit itself bears witness with our spirit that we are children of God, and if children, then heirs, heirs of God and joint heirs with Christ, if only we suffer with him so that we may also be glorified with him" (Rom 8:16–17). To enjoy the company of Christ in heaven, all on earth should implore the help of Mary, Refuge of Sinners. This gracious Lady receives those disposed to become her spiritual children; those who find themselves not so disposed, she softens.

In addition to Penance and Reconciliation, the Church offers another sacrament of healing, the Anointing of the Sick. This holy anointing supplies a remedy, as Saint Thomas Aquinas expresses it, "against those elements of sin which remain, those namely which, whether through negligence or ignorance, are not sufficiently removed by penance."[14] For reasons that cultural practices may explain, many people today have forgotten that the dying process brings its own fears and unknowns. These arise, for instance, from the natural regret and remorse for wrongdoings that, at the hour of death, may intensify. The Anointing of the Sick reminds Christian believers that their time for actively participating in their own redemption nears its end. The special kind of forgiveness and healing that holy anointing imparts persuades Catholics to request (or have requested for them) the Anointing of the Sick as they approach the moment of death. Nobody, especially when burdened by serious illness, can shake off attachment to every sin. Clinging to  sin, however, does not prepare one to encounter the thrice-Holy God. This sacrament removes the residual "elements" of even confessed sins. So the Church teaches that the Anointing of the Sick numbers among its effects "the forgiveness of sins, if the sick person was not able to obtain it through the sacrament of Penance."[15] What alternative exists to this beneficent

sacramental mediation? Dead sinners spend time in Purgatory.

Mary's fifth sorrow emphasizes her closeness to sinners. She hears Christ exclaim, "Father, 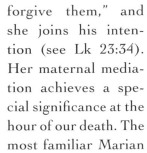 forgive them," and she joins his intention (see Lk 23:34). Her maternal mediation achieves a special significance at the hour of our death. The most familiar Marian prayer, the Hail Mary, explicitly asks for her intercession "now and at the hour of our death. Amen." Religious orders, such as the Dominicans, customarily sing the *Salve Regina* at the deathbed of their dying members. These and many other Catholic practices urge us to seek the full sacramental mediation of Christ's Passion and death at that moment when one's physical condition portends death. Of course, the Church also promises that the Anointing of the Sick may result in "the restoration of health, if it is conducive to the salvation of his soul." This surprising fruit of the sacrament points up the importance that Catholics should attach to remaining faithful to their baptismal promises.

The prophet Zechariah foretells: "On that day there will no longer be cold or frost. There will be one continuous day — it is known to the LORD — not day and night, for in the evening there will be light" (Zec 14:6–7). The poet Claudel ponders the word "frost" — in the Vulgate Latin, *gelu*. He strikingly observes that at the moment of Christ's death "everything congeals into a certain exorbitant state that at once sparks both vigilance and astonishment."[16] His meditation suits those who are near death, especially. Given the magnitude of this moment in the world's history, the *Stabat Mater* properly reserves this fifth sorrow of Mary to recall the prophecy of Simeon: "Whose soul, lamenting, / sorrowing and grieving, / has been pierced by the sword."[17]

THE SIXTH SWORD:
MARY RECEIVES
THE BODY OF JESUS IN HER ARMS

"When it was evening, there came a rich man from Arimathea named Joseph, who was himself a disciple of Jesus. He went to Pilate and asked for the body of Jesus; then Pilate ordered it to be handed over. Taking the body, Joseph wrapped it [in] clean linen . . ."

(Mt 27:57–59)

In churches and in museums everywhere, one sees representations of the Pietà. Mary holds the dead body of her Son. The white marble sculpture by Michelangelo that sits in Saint Peter's Basilica ranks among the best known. These images of Our Lady cradling Christ's dead body take their inspiration from what the

Scriptures record about the initiative of a certain New Testament figure, Joseph of Arimathea: "When it was already evening, since it was the day of preparation, the day before the sabbath, Joseph of Arimathea, a distinguished member of the council, who was himself awaiting the kingdom of God, came and courageously went to Pilate and asked for the body of Jesus." The Gospel of Mark continues: "Pilate was amazed that he was already dead. He summoned the centurion and asked him if Jesus had already died. And when he learned of it from the centurion, he gave the body to Joseph" (Mk 15:42–45). The Evangelist leaves us wondering what happened next. The Christian tradition responds by posing a rhetorical question: into whose arms would this pious Arimathean confide so precious a body if not those of Christ's mother? Mary's sixth sorrow completes, in a certain sense, all that Simeon foretold about her participation in the dolorous destiny of her Child. After the moment of the Pietà, Mary will hand over the body of her Son to those devout persons who will bury him.

Mary holds carefully the dead body of Christ, "which even after death remained united to the divine person of Christ."[1] She protects it as she did when "she wrapped him in swaddling clothes and laid him in a manger" (Lk 2:7). Christological readings of the Old Testament associate Mary with Rizpah, the mother of King Saul's sons Armoni and Meribbaal. Rizpah

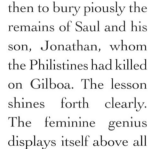

carefully protected their dead bodies after David had allowed them both to be killed by the Gibeonites in order to satisfy a blood feud: "Then Rizpah, Aiah's daughter, took sackcloth and spread it out for herself on the rock from the beginning of the harvest until rain came down on them from the heavens, fending off the birds of the heavens from settling on them by day, and the wild animals by night" (2 Sam 21:10). The Second Book of Samuel goes on to relate that Rizpah's maternal solicitude for the bodies of her dead sons moved David first to obtain and then to bury piously the remains of Saul and his son, Jonathan, whom the Philistines had killed on Gilboa. The lesson shines forth clearly. The feminine genius displays itself above all in compassion and piety. In these virtues, women lead the way. In this context, Mary's piety refers to a strong virtue of her soul, not an ephemeral disposition of spirit. Mary's sixth sorrow exhibits—as the dual meaning in Italian of *pietà* reminds us—both pity and piety.

Because of her participation in the sorrows of Calvary, the Church invokes Mary as Queen of Martyrs. As the First Eucharistic Prayer shows, the Church has from the earliest centuries named, alongside the Apostles and early Popes, those virgin martyrs—some of whom suffered even as young teenagers—who sacrificed their lives for Christ: Felicity, Perpetua, Agatha, Lucy, Agnes, Cecilia, Anastasia. . . . No period in the life of the Church escapes persecution and suffering. Mary's sixth sorrow prepares us to face the difficult circumstances that arise in our own lives. She consoles us with the knowledge that no suffering occurs outside of the overarching plan of the divine wisdom and goodness. The Pietà comforts the world. For whether Christian martyr or not, no human person escapes the ultimate suffering, death.

Funerals form an integral part of Catholic life and liturgy. The *Catechism of the Catholic Church* explains the profound significance that the Church attaches to our conducting the proper religious ceremonies around the body of a deceased person: "The ministry of the Church in this instance aims at expressing efficacious communion with the deceased, at the participation in that communion of the community gathered for the funeral, and at the proclamation of eternal life to the community."[2] The evocative image that belongs to Mary's sixth sorrow—an image also venerated under the title of Our Lady of Compassion, for example, in the celebrated church of Notre Dame des Ardilliers at Saumur in the valley of the Loire River—incarnates Catholic teaching about how one ought to act after the death of a friend or family member. In a word, we should attend to their bodies. Though the dead body of Christ was unlike a mortal corpse, Mary's receiving the dead body of her Son strikingly represents the communion that the Church of the living enjoys with those of her members who have died. Does she experience sorrow? Of course, she does! What is important for the Christian to recall? Mary does not flee the sorrow. She embraces it.

How may one express the Christian's "communion with the deceased"? We should remember that suffrages or the offering of prayers for the dead shape Catholic devotion and *pietà*. The Commemoration of All the Faithful Departed, sometimes known as All Souls Day, affords an annual opportunity to display this compassion and piety. The anniversary of the death of a loved one provides another occasion when we can pray for and renew our communion with the departed. Some Catholic people observe the thirtieth, sixtieth, and ninetieth day anniversaries of a person's death. English-speaking Catholics recall the practice of requesting a "Month's Mind" Mass for a deceased person. Many other pious activities, for instance, enrollment in recognized Purgatorial Societies, afford Catholic people the means to profess their communion with those who have preceded them in death. Catholic devotion toward the dead excludes superstitious practices. Instead, prayer for the repose of a dead person's soul supplies Catholics the opportunity to prolong the pity and the piety that Mary's sixth sorrow encourages. The practices of praying for the dead teach the hearts of the living faithful to love the things of heaven.

Communion with the faithful departed occurs during every Mass. Each of the Eucharistic Prayers includes a memento for the dead. Sometimes, such as at funeral Masses, the liturgical text even provides for the priest's mentioning the deceased person's name. Catholic priests offer Mass for both the living and the dead. "It is in the Eucharistic cult or in the Eucharistic assembly of the faithful (*synaxis*) that they [priests] . . . unite the votive offerings of the faithful to the sacrifice of Christ their head."[3] A long-standing custom among the Catholic faithful stipulates that those persons who request a special intention for a Mass should make an offering to the Church. These (usually) monetary offerings contribute to the material support of the priest. Such nominal offerings also afford Catholics a concrete and specific way to express fitting compassion and piety toward the faithful departed, especially those who were known to them.

∼

The place that the priest holds in the Eucharistic assembly suggests the task that is given to those in Holy Orders. Priests seek to unite the Catholic people, whether living or dead, into the one communion of the Church. Priests pastor their people. Like good shepherds, they keep before their eyes the prayer that Christ prayed on the night before he died: "that they may all be one" (Jn 17:21). It should come as no surprise, then, that the defect that the sacrament of Holy

Orders works to remove concerns the fragmentation of community. Specifically, Holy Orders exists to guard against a breakup of the many who form the Catholic communion. Saint Thomas Aquinas laconically expresses this defect that Holy Orders addresses in two Latin words: "dissolutionem multitudinis."[4] More recently, the pope and bishops have set before us a simi-

lar theme: "In the Church and on behalf of the Church, priests are a sacramental representation of Jesus Christ, the Head and Shepherd . . . showing his loving concern to the point of a total gift of self for the flock, which they gather into unity and lead to the Father through Christ and in the Spirit."[5] As the repeated calls for worldwide evangelization make clear, no person on the face of the earth stands excluded from belonging to this privileged "flock."

In order to appreciate the importance of the remedy that Holy Orders sets in motion, the Catholic people should recall that the Church, even after the Second Vatican Council, has never taught that ecumenical and inter-religious dialogues invite us to embrace religious relativism. As experience has shown, diversity of religious practices and beliefs divides the human community, even though the Church looks for proper ways to encourage tolerance. Within the Christian community itself, sin divides friend from friend. Sin always requires a remedy. While the right kind of human interventions may assist the remedying of sinful behavior, only God's grace heals and uplifts the sinner. This grace ordinarily is given in the confessional. Priests administer the other sacraments, and so they supply instrumentally the remedies that these sacraments bestow. In order to ease divisions within the human community, the world needs priests. The collegial nature of

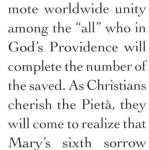

priestly ministry (in the Church of faith and sacraments) displays the unity that priests foster.[6] They foster this unity among the "many" of the Catholic community; they promote worldwide unity among the "all" who in God's Providence will complete the number of the saved. As Christians cherish the Pietà, they will come to realize that Mary's sixth sorrow sustains the Church, especially her priests, until the end of time: "When everything is subjected to [Christ], then the Son himself will [also] be subjected to the one who subjected everything to him, so that God may be all in all" (1 Cor 15:28). The ministrations of priests prepare us for this final, glorious subjection.

Priests, like Mary, occupy a privileged position among the

mediations that God has established in the Church of Christ. Priests learn from Mary that though they serve as living instruments of God's love, they never stand between their people and God. As Pope Francis has reminded the Christian world, the priest is a "mediator not an intermediary."[7] Nothing, in any case, can interpose itself between God and the human creature He has created. At the same time, the priest remains a true and indispensable mediator, and there exists no replacement either for him or for what he does. For, within the logic of the Incarnation, no human person can sustain an unmediated relationship with God. The Book of Proverbs recounts that "Wisdom

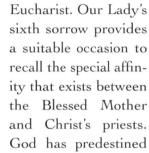

has prepared her meat, mixed her wine, yes, she has spread her table" (Prov 9:2). Spiritual authors interpret this text as referring, variously and variously, to Mary and to the Eucharist. Our Lady's sixth sorrow provides a suitable occasion to recall the special affinity that exists between the Blessed Mother and Christ's priests. God has predestined Mary and priests to handle, albeit diversely, that is, physically or sacramentally, the Body of Christ. Just as one could never tell the story of the Cross of Christ without reference to the Sorrowful Mother, so the practice of true religion would be impossible without the sacred ministry of the priest.

THE SEVENTH SWORD: THE BODY OF JESUS IS PLACED IN THE TOMB

"They took the body of Jesus and bound it with burial cloths along with the spices, according to the Jewish burial custom. Now in the place where he had been crucified there was a garden, and in the garden a new tomb, in which no one had yet been buried. So they laid Jesus there because of the Jewish preparation day; for the tomb was close by."

(Jn 19:40–42)

ary's seventh sorrow heralds a certain denouement in the drama of our redemption. Those who have read the New Testament know that the burial of Jesus provides a juncture, as it were, between Mary's sorrows and her joys. At the same time, as the last verse that we read in the Gospel of Matthew about Christ's burial makes plain, his entombment brings its own moment of finality: "Then [Joseph of Arimathea] rolled a huge stone across the entrance to the tomb and departed" (Mt 27:60). Anyone who has closed a casket or has left the freshly opened grave site of a loved one understands the human emotion that Our Lady underwent once she saw that the "huge stone" was

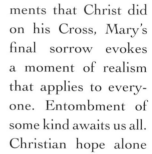

in place. Because of her remaining with Jesus until the end, we venerate this emotion as her seventh and last sorrow. Although many will not suffer the same torments that Christ did on his Cross, Mary's final sorrow evokes a moment of realism that applies to everyone. Entombment of some kind awaits us all. Christian hope alone offers an escape from the finality of the tomb. We find this sentiment reflected in the last stanza of the *Stabat Mater*: "When my body dies, / let my soul be given / the glory of paradise. Amen."[1] This hope for glory, however, comes only as a gift of Christ's grace.

Gustave Doré, in his engraving *La mort d'Agag*, captures a frightening scene from the Old

Testament. This illustration—one of more than two hundred in Doré's *La Sainte Bible*—shows the prophet Samuel ordering the execution of a foreign king who had wrought injury and death on Israel.[2] The biblical text that inspired the artist expresses the pathos of the moment: "Samuel commanded, 'Bring Agag, king of Amalek, to me.' Agag came to him struggling and saying, 'So it is bitter death!'" (1 Sam 15:32). Before the Resurrection of the Lord, no other reaction to death would have been possible. *Amara mors*. Bitter death. These words come from the mouth of a man whose armies God himself commanded Israel to engage in combat. Still, what Agag utters provides a more honest glimpse of how those

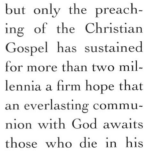

without faith think about death than do the romantic euphemisms we hear from today's cultivated secularists. One can easily fabricate mythologies about life after death, but only the preaching of the Christian Gospel has sustained for more than two millennia a firm hope that an everlasting communion with God awaits those who die in his friendship. Whenever Christians recite the Apostles' Creed they are reminded of this hope: "I believe in ... the resurrection of the body, and life everlasting. Amen."[3] Because of this supernatural hope, Christians pray confidently for deliverance from a bitter death.

The seventh sorrow of Mary reminds us of an ancient liturgical piece that expresses a proper

Christian outlook on death. The first line of the Latin text identifies the antiphon, *Media vita in morte sumus*, which has echoed since the mid-eighth century through cathedral chancels and monastery cloisters. The biographers of Saint Thomas Aquinas report that when he heard this antiphon sung in chapel, he was moved to tears of supplication.[4]

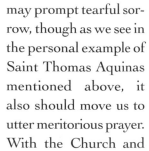

When we remain in the company of Mary, especially as she stands at the tomb of her Son, we make this plea for divine mercy our own: "In the midst of life we be in death: / Of whom may we seek for succour, but of Thee, / O Lord, which for our sins art justly displeased? / Yet, O Lord God most holy, O Lord most mighty, / O holy and most merciful Saviour, / Deliver us not into the bitter pains of eternal death."[5] The Amalekian king, Agag, struggled with his ordained fate. For the Christian who awaits his own resurrection, the thought of a burial may prompt tearful sorrow, though as we see in the personal example of Saint Thomas Aquinas mentioned above, it also should move us to utter meritorious prayer. With the Church and her saints, we also plead for deliverance from the "bitter pains of eternal death."

"They took the body of Jesus and bound it with burial cloths along with the spices, according to the Jewish burial custom" (Jn 19:40). The Church encourages us to sustain our meditation on Mary's sorrows until this moment when, according to the practices they inherited from Israel, Christ's disciples reverence the dead body of Jesus. In other words, they give him a proper burial. Mary's seventh sorrow should incline us to imitate this reverence. Today, the Church instructs us about how to treat the bodies of our deceased: "The bodies of the dead must be treated with 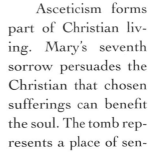 respect and charity, in faith and hope of the Resurrection. The burial of the dead is a corporal work of mercy; it honors the children of God, who are temples of the Holy Spirit."[6] Our meditation on the last of Mary's sorrows should come to mind when we find ourselves faced with the opportunity to exercise this corporal work of mercy. This final meditation also shows us that accompanying a dead body to its final resting place can spark salutary thoughts in both Christian believers and those without faith in the Resurrection.

Asceticism forms part of Christian living. Mary's seventh sorrow persuades the Christian that chosen sufferings can benefit the soul. The tomb represents a place of sensory deprivation. True enough, Christian mortification ordinarily takes this form: fasting and almsgiving require that we relinquish an undue attachment to food and money. On the other hand, the American novelist Nathaniel Hawthorne (1804–64), though not a Catholic, showed his penetration into the spiritual meaning of ascetical practices when he engaged in conversation a Martha Vineyard's tombstone engraver, a certain Mr. Wigglesworth. The sculptor, as Hawthorne deferentially referred to this old Yankee, took pride in his sepulchral work. For his part, however, Hawthorne felt obliged to opine that "to gain the truer conception of DEATH, I would forget the GRAVE!"[7] Though the engraver may have demurred at this apparent slight to his craft, Hawthorne was correct: to gain a proper appreciation for ascetical practices—mortifications, or "little deaths"—we need to look beyond them.

Mary's seventh sorrow places her in an "in-between time." Those who believe in what happened very "early" on Easter morning recognize that Christ's burial inaugurates a transitional period for his Mother (see Jn 20:1). Her Good Friday compassion gives way to her Holy Saturday waiting. Now, Mary finds herself bereft but not without hope.

Like the body of Christ that does not suffer corruption in the grave, Mary's sorrow reaches its stasis or equilibrium. She waits for that early morning Easter sunrise, that *valde mane*, which, according to traditional Marian piety, she never doubted would take place.

∽

Among the blessings that have followed the close of the Second Vatican Council in 1965, one must include the rich instruction on Christian marriage that the pontificate of Saint John Paul II (1978–2005) provided the Church. The positive tone of the holy Pope's instruction has encouraged even married persons outside of the Catholic communion. At the same time, his instruction on marriage and family never failed to insist upon the proper relationship between fruitfulness and that pleasure which accompanies the acts proper to spouses. Prima facie, it may appear odd to speak about Matrimony in association with Mary's sorrows, especially her seventh sorrow. Marriage stands at the opposite pole from the tomb. When, however, we ponder what the sacrament of Matrimony aims to remedy in a fallen human race, we discover some surprising resonances with Mary's seventh sorrow.

The perennial instruction about marriage tells us that the sacrament of Matrimony provides a remedy against intemperate lust and also makes good, according to classical theology, "the losses in the community incurred through death."[8] These two remedies appear in the Church's authoritative explanation of marriage: "The matrimonial covenant, by which a man and a woman establish between themselves a partnership of the whole of life, is by its nature ordered toward the good of the spouses and the procreation and education of offspring; this covenant between baptized persons has been raised by Christ the Lord to the dignity of a sacrament."[9] Certain contemporary outlooks on marriage tend to minimize the place that the procreation of offspring plays in sustaining husband and wife. While the Church regards married life as an altogether unique means of sanctification for the couple, the procreation and education of children, as every parent realizes, includes its own share of sorrow. Mary's sorrow at the tomb encourages married couples to see that God has ordained their intimacies to serve the survival of the human race. Christian mothers and fathers of course rejoice not only because they have helped to replenish the population, but especially because they know that the children born to them inherit, through Baptism, the promise of eternal life.

Married couples take great solace from their devotion to Our Lady. They recognize in her both spouse and mother. Mary's virginity encourages them. Throughout Christian history mystical authors have mined the Song of Songs—in older translations, the Canticle of Canticles—for clues about the divine intimacy. One verse, "I belong to my lover, and my lover belongs to me; / he feeds among the lilies" (Sg 6:3), especially drew forth profound commentaries about loving God. Commonly, Christian interpreters of the Song have identified the bride with the human soul and the bridegroom with Christ, who, because of his perfect chastity, "feeds among the lilies." Throughout the Song of Songs, both bride and bridegroom express their longing to embrace each other. Married couples bring their own understanding to this longing. Because of the virtuous intimacies that married couples share, they find themselves in a position to discover spiritual truths in the Song of Songs that celibate clerics or chaste religious may not recognize. To benefit from what they learn about the sanctifying power of married love, Christian couples must join Mary at the tomb. Married life, as many have come to

appreciate, involves patient and sometimes sorrowful waiting. Who better can sustain married couples than the Mother whose sorrows never overshadowed her enlightened faith and, indeed, her joy. Because "his left hand is under my head / and his right arm embraces me" (Sg 8:3), the Mother of Christ knows grief but never sadness.

CONCLUSION

wo deeply Catholic sentiments expressed in consecutive stanzas of the *Stabat Mater* bring these meditations on Mary's sorrow to completion. The first of these stanzas expresses what should be the strong inclination of those who acknowledge their sins;[1] the second proposes a way of life:[2]

Make me truly weep with you,
grieving with Him who is crucified
so that I may live.

To stand by the cross with you,
to be freely joined with you
in lamentation, I desire.

God allows no Christian to bypass sharing in Mary's sorrows. Since he did not protect the Immaculate Mother of His Son from the Seven Sorrows that the Church commemorates, why would he exempt those who have inherited the ancient guilt of Adam and Eve? We, indeed, as Proverbs affirms, fall daily: "the just fall seven times" (Prov 24:16). The Christian believer, then, who follows the rhythms set by the Church's preaching, sacraments, and devotional life never outgrows his or her need for returning to Our Lady of Sorrows.

In Catholic usage, seven represents the perfect number for things of this earth. One finds it odd to consider perfect sorrow, especially in an age when people do everything to eliminate suffering and sorrow. As much as anyone, Christian believers work to relieve worldly sufferings. Meditating on Mary's perfect Seven Sorrows brings comfort to those "weeping in this valley of tears." Even more, however, those believers who discover the mystery that the Seven Sorrows of Mary proclaim enjoy an advantage. These blessed souls realize that the Mother of Sorrows stands ready to transform into little sacraments of redemption those sufferings which escape our best efforts to assuage them.

The seven sacraments heal the wounds of sin and thereby ready us for worship. We worship God best through the sacraments. Each of the Church's sacraments requires the involvement of a priest. Sometimes suitable young men shy away from pursuing the priesthood because they fear the

affective solitude that inevitably intrudes into the life of the celibate Catholic priest. By accompanying them in their ministries, Our Lady of Sorrows supplies a maternal remedy for the felt solitude that can haunt a priest. Those who cherish devotion to Mary's Seven Sorrows willingly intercede for priests and for priestly vocations. Without the ministry of priests, we would find ourselves bereft of the remedies that God has ordained to heal the wounds of sin. Let us all, then, priest and laity alike, make this plea from the *Stabat Mater* our frequent invocation:[3]

Holy Mother, bring this to pass,
transfix the wounds of Him
who is crucified
firmly onto my heart.

Notes

The First Sword: The Prophecy of Simeon

[1] Encyclical Letter of Pope John Paul II *Redemptoris Mater*, no. 18.

[2] Oscar Wilde, *The Ballad of Reading Gaol*, IV (New York: Brentano's, 1909).

[3] See for example, Sergei Nikolaevich Bulgakov, *Churchly Joy: Orthodox Devotions for the Church Year*, trans. Boris Jakim (Grand Rapids, MI: Wm. B. Eerdmans, 2008), pp. 10-11.

[4] *Catechism of the Catholic Church (CCC)*, Frontispiece, Part Two.

[5] David Bourke, *The Sacraments*, vol. 56, Blackfriars *Summa Theologiae* (New York: McGraw-Hill Book Company, 1975), p. 142n "d."

[6] Encyclical Letter of Pope Francis *Lumen fidei*, no. 42.

[7] In *Summa Theologiae* III, q. 65, art. 1, Aquinas sums up the anterior tradition.

[8] *Lumen fidei*, no. 42.

[9] See the Encyclical Letter *Fides et ratio*, no. 53: "The [First Vatican] Council began with the basic criterion, presupposed by Revelation itself, of the natural knowability of the existence of God, the beginning and end of all things, and concluded with the solemn assertion quoted earlier: 'There are two orders of knowledge, distinct not only in their point of departure, but also in their object'."

[10] See *Summa Theologiae* III, q. 69, art. 9, ad 1.

The Second Sword: The Flight into Egypt

[1] C. S. Lewis, *God in the Dock*, ed. W. Hooper (London: Geoffrey Bles, 1971). In the practice of the English courts, the "dock" refers to the place where persons on trial are made to stand as their cases are judged.

[2] Saint Quodvultdeus (*Sermo 2 de Symbolo:* PL 40, 655) as found in *The Liturgy of the Hours*, Office of Readings for the Feast of the Holy Innocents on December 28.

[3] The 1657 painting may be seen in the Musée des Beaux-Arts de Lyon.

[4] Gerald Vann, O.P., *The Seven Swords* (New York: Sheed and Ward, 1953), p. 27. Father Vann cites Aquinas's Latin: "Voluit fugere ut fugientes a facie Dei revocaret" (*Lectura super Matthaeum*, chap. 2). My enumeration of Mary's sorrows as seven swords follows the pattern of his book.

[5] See *Summa Theologiae* II-II, q. 19, arts. 3 & 4.

[6] *CCC*, no. 2354.

[7] In *Summa Theologiae* III, q. 65, art. 1, Aquinas actually says, "to which the soul is subject for some little time after birth."

[8] See the "Morbidity and Mortality Weekly Report" (MMWR) on the website for the Centers for Disease Control and Prevention.

The Third Sword: The Loss of the Child Jesus in the Temple

[1] *Roman Missal*, Profession of Faith, the Niceno-Constantinopolitan Creed.

[2] "Get Happy" was composed by Harold Arlen, with lyrics written by Ted Koehler. Ella Fitzgerald recorded the song in her album "Ella Fitzgerald Sings the Harold Arlen Songbook."

[3] See Guy Gaucher, *The Passion of Thérèse of Lisieux*, trans. Sr. Anne Marie Brennan, O.C.D. (New York: Crossroad, 1990), p. 229, citing *Derniers Entretiens* (6 July, no. 4): "Our Lord enjoyed all the delights of the Trinity when he was in the garden of Olives, and still his agony was none the less cruel. It's a mystery, but I assure you that I understand something of it from what I'm experiencing myself."

[4] See, for example, *Story of a Soul. The Autobiography of St. Thérèse of Lisieux*, trans. John Clarke, O.C.D. (Washington, DC: ICS Publications, 1976), p. 157: "My desire for suffering was answered, and yet my attraction for it did not diminish. My soul soon shared in the sufferings of my heart. Spiritual aridity was my daily bread and, deprived of all consolation, I was still the happiest of creatures since all my desires had been satisfied."

[5] *Lumen fidei*, no. 7.

[6] *Summa Theologiae* III, q. 79, art. 4. The quotation comes from Saint Ambrose's *On the Sacraments*.

[7] See, for example, Jacques-Bénigne Bossuet (1627–1704), *Méditations sur l'Evangile, . . . la Cène, 57ème jour* (Paris, 1731).

The Fourth Sword: Mary Meets Jesus on the Way to Calvary

[1] *Redemptoris Mater*, no. 26.

[2] Modern devotion to the Stations of the Cross found impetus from the preaching of the Franciscan priest Saint Leonard of Port Maurice, who persuaded Pope Benedict XIV (1740–58) to set up Stations of the Cross in the Coliseum.

[3] The Vatican Today, News.Va: "Vatican City, 15 March 2012 (VIS) — The texts for meditation during this year's Way of the Cross, to be held at the Colosseum on Good Friday, have, by order of the Holy Father, been written by Danilo and Anna Maria Zanzucchi, a married couple and founders of the New Families Movement, which is part of the 'Focolari' Movement."

[4] *CCC*, no. 796.

[5] *Summa Theologiae* I-II, q. 36, art. 1.

[6] For a discussion, see *Summa Theologiae* I-II, q. 35, art. 2. English translations of Saint Thomas's Latin differ. What is important to observe is that Aquinas makes *tristitia* (what I translate as sadness) a species of *dolor* (what I translate as pain or grief).

[7] "O quam tristis et afflicta / Fuit illa benedicta / Mater unigeniti." Various versions of the *Stabat Mater* exist in both Latin and English (see

Notes

http://www.stabatmater.info/english.html).
For the present anonymous translation see
http://www.arvopart.org/composition_text.
php?id=2 [accessed 8 August 2013]. Catholic devotional usage favors the translation by the English convert and Birmingham Oratorian Father Edward Caswall, which appears in *Lyra Catholica* (1849).

[8] For instance, see Y.-M. Congar, "Cajetan et la dévotion à la Compassion de Marie: L'opuscule 'De Spasimo,'" *La vie spirituelle, ascétique et mystique* 38 (1934): pp. 142–160.

[9] Vann, *Seven Swords*, p. 46.

[10] "Queen of the May" (aka "Bring Flowers of the Rarest") by Mary E. Walsh (1883); based on the traditional thirteenth-century Catholic hymn.

[11] See *CCC*, no. 1497.

[12] *CCC*, no. 1459.

[13] Paul Claudel, *L'Épée et le Miroir* (Paris: Gallimard, 1939), p. 48: "de cette nuit qui s'est refusé à Le connaître et à qui, à défaut d'un regard, Il n'a emprunté ques Ses larmes!"

[14] See *CCC*, no. 1432.

The Fifth Sword: Jesus Dies on the Cross

[1] "Stabat mater dolorosa / Juxta crucem lacrymosa / Dum pendebat Filius."

[2] Second Vatican Ecumenical Council, Dogmatic Constitution on the Church *Lumen gentium*, no. 58.

[3] *Redemptoris Mater*, nos. 17, 18.

[4] *Collection of Masses of the Blessed Virgin Mary*, Preface of the Mass of the Blessed Virgin Mary, Mother and Mediatrix of Grace (*Beata Maria Virgo, Mater et Mediatrix Gratiæ*).

[5] *Lumen gentium*, no. 62.

[6] *Redemptoris Mater*, no. 38.

[7] For example, the seventeenth-century Spanish Dominican priest and Thomist theologian Peter de Godoy (†1677) writes: "Because the Head of the Church bespeaks not only perfection and superabundance but also an influx of condign merits, which the Blessed Virgin as a member of the Church did not possess; therefore she is not called the head, but the Neck of the Church inasmuch as she is more joined [than others] to Christ the head."

[8] Claudel, *L'Épée*, p. 86.

[9] *Redemptionis Mater*, no. 48.

[10] *Œuvres complètes de saint Louie-Marie Grignion de Montfort* (*Paris: Aux Éditions du Seuil*, 1966), *Amour de la Sagesse Eternelle*, no. 207, p. 206: "il descend aucun don céleste sur la terre qu'il ne passe pas elle [Marie] comme par un canal."

[11] *Roman Missal*, "The Easter Vigil in the Holy Night, Renewal of Baptismal Promises."

[12] The modern version of this prayer received an indulgence from Pope Pius IX in 1846.

[13] Vann, *Seven Swords*, p. 58.

[14] *Summa Theologiae* III, q. 65, art. 1.

[15] *CCC*, no. 1532.

[16] Claudel, *L'Épée*, p. 83: "Tout se coagule dans un certain état exorbitant à la fois de vigilance et de stupor."

[17] "Cujus animam gementem / Contristatem et dolentes / Pertransivit gladius."

The Sixth Sword: Mary Receives the Body of Jesus in Her Arms

[1] *CCC*, no. 650.

[2] *CCC*, no.1684.

[3] *CCC*, no. 1566.

[4] *Summa Theologiae* III, q. 65, art. 1.

[5] Post-synodal Apostolic Exhortation *Pastores dabo vobis*, no. 15.

[6] See *CCC*, no. 877: "It belongs to the sacramental nature of ecclesial ministry that it have a collegial character. In fact, from the beginning of his ministry, the Lord Jesus instituted the Twelve as 'the seeds of the new Israel and the beginning of the sacred hierarchy.' Chosen together, they were also sent out together, and their fraternal unity would be at the service of the fraternal communion of all the faithful: they would reflect and witness to the communion of the divine persons."

[7] Homily of Pope Francis, Saint Peter's Basilica, Holy Thursday, 28 March 2013: "Those who do not go out of themselves, instead of being mediators, gradually become intermediaries, managers."

The Seventh Sword: The Body of Jesus Is Placed in the Tomb

[1] "Quando corpus morietur / Fac ut animae donetur / Paradisi gloria. Amen."

[2] From Doré's *La Sainte Bible*, according to the Vulgate, new translation (Tours: Mame, 1866).

[3] *Roman Missal*, "The Apostles' Creed."

[4] See Jean-Pierre Torrell, O.P., *Saint Thomas Aquinas*, vol. 1, *The Person and His Work*, trans. Robert Royal (Washington, DC: The Catholic University of America Press, rev. ed. 2005), p. 288, n. 101.

[5] English translation, from the *Book of Common Prayer*, of the medieval Latin: "Media vita in morte sumus / Quem quaerimus adjutorem nisi te, Domine? / Qui pro peccatis nostris juste irasceris / Sancte Deus, Sancte fortis, / Sancte et misericors Salvator, / Amaræ morti ne tradas nos."

[6] *CCC*, no. 2300.

[7] Nathaniel Hawthorne, "Chippings With a Chisel," which was originally published in *The Democratic Review* 9 (Sept. 1838), pp. 18-26, and again in his *Twice Told Tales*. His daughter, Rose Hawthorne, converted to Catholicism and eventually founded a congregation of Dominican nuns to care for the terminally ill.

[8] *Summa Theologiae* III, q. 65, art. 1.

[9] *CCC*, no. 1601, citing the *Code of Canon Law*, can. 1055 §1.

Notes

Conclusion

---

[1] "Fac me vere tecum flere / Crucifixo condolere / Donec ego vixero."

[2] "Juxta crucem tecum stare / Te libenter sociare / In planctu desidero."

[3] "Sancta Mater istud agas / Crucifixi fige plagas / Corde meo valide."

www.magnificat.com